INFINITICS

A BEST WAY TO INFINITY

GUNEET RATNANI

To my family and Nature

Contents

Foreword

This book gives a proper idea about an Infinity and times while dealing with operations and calculations related to Infinities made on the basis of cantor's theorem and Hyperreal numbers. This also talks about various types of Infinities and some imperfect divisions. It also talks about restrictions regarding 0 and 0 over 0. Here Infinity is treated like an actual number (not as variable) with a reason but not as a finite number, thus resulting into many infinities. It is an important topic for the field of the mathematics as it craves accuracy.

Acknowledgements

I would like to express my deepest gratitude to Arvind Sir, who ignited my curiosity about infinity and fostered my love for mathematics.

I am also incredibly thankful to Tejas for being the very first reader of this book.

CHAPTER ONE

INTRODUCTION

Let Infinitics be the <u>branch of mathematics</u> which deals about the basic concepts of Infinities and operations performed related to Infinity.

Infinity, in general, is a space or time without any end. And in mathematics, the number that is larger than any other natural number that we can imagine or think of.

From Georg Cantor's theorem, we obtain an unlimited hierarchy of Infinite cardinals, in which each set is strictly bigger than the last one. Since this theorem implies that there is no largest cardinal number (Cantor, 1891).

Hence we know Infinity what we have thought of as THE full stop of the number series but there's no largest cardinal number and an infinite set can be bigger than other infinite set. Thus, shouldn't be 'not defined'? I know you will think Infinity is not a number and all and we will get on that later in this book.

Cantor's views were accepted worldwide and someplaces in mathematics considering infinity as a number has become fruitful for some and knowing that in various places, some mathematicians think that there is a variable which is tending towards infinity but isn't infinity because if we take equal to infinity then we are defining it as we don't know what is infinity exactly besides the definitions like being the largest number, endless and limitless.

Infinity number is under Hyperreal number system which is growing infinitely and as no upper bound (in Infinitics, it is simply called as <u>Infinity or Infinite Number or Infinity Number</u>).

Infinity can behave like a number in terms of a variable, is concluded by Hyperreal number system (Robinson, 1966) which means that there is no biggest Hyperreal number and which is like there is no largest Infinity out there which Cantor's theorem also says.

It also states that Infinite and Infinitesimal as number where we can perform operations with them like addition, multiplication, etc which Infinitics also agrees on but also argues on.

Conclusion of this introduction:-

1) Since Infinite set contain Infinite elements and two different Infinite sets can also different in size. Thus we can conclude from that two Infinities can also differ in their size or there are bigger Infinities than one another and from the statement 'there is no largest cardinal number'.

2) Infinity is a number in today's Mathematics.

3) Comparsion of two Infinite sets can be done.

CHAPTER TWO

BETA INFINITY

Before starting this topic, let's forget about what is 1/0, what gives an Infinity and which is 'Not defined' for a while and now let's start from the beginning and a basic logic for an Infinity.

Infinity is something that if we start writing it, it never stops (in terms of numbers). Let's take an example, 1000.... Here, if we starts writing zeros on the right hand side and never stops (A hypothetical assumption since we can't do that) or if I take a number '1' and starts multiplying it with '10' and never stop (Hypothetically), we will have our Infinity, as it also matches the definition of an Infinity, having no limit, endless and has it infinite digits.

It's like when you starts summing 1+1+1+1+.... (where number of terms are endless), it will give us an Infinity. Similarly, if we starting multiplying with 10 without an end of it, it will lead to an another Infinity.

Here if we see that we are writing zeros on the right hand side on the 1 is with some rate so the given infinity 1000.... increases with some rate?. But 1000... is Infinity and you will think that how come an Infinity is connected with rate ?

Let's talk about when we tell a computer to write an Infinity and we see that it starts repeating zeros or a specific number or random numbers over and over again, as infinity has infinite digits. A number is printed at an instant by a computer which is finite by digits and in reality infinity can't be printed all in once as it is infinite by digits but if we tell computer to write a number which has one Million digits it will print at once which is a very big number so, it seems to be pointing that, Non fixed Infinite has it's rate of increasing BUT we know it's not in reality.

But also in mathematics considering infinity with a rate is found to be very fruitful and it has various applications also (in the mathematical operation also) and we will discuss about it later on. Note that I'm not saying that Infinity (Infinite) has slow rate of increasing or normal or very very large. since, we don't know it's exact value let's consider it 'X' for a while.

The people may think that Infinity when considered with rate at some unit time, the infinity will look like a finite number at every single unit time, but we know that Infinity is not finite numbers at different unit times but as said in reality, Infinity doesn't come with a rate but here Infinities gives us idea to think of an Infinity with a rate to simply perform operation on Infinities and Infinitesimal {And in reality, Infinity increases at time = 0 second to 0 second i.e. 'X' = Not defined, which we all can agree on} and which also doesn't mean Infinity doesn't grow with unit time. So in Infinitics, when we are considering it with a rate, the definitions changes for a finite and Infinite number.

{The extra zeros which come before and after (after in decimal) a finite number which has doesn't change the meaning or the value of that finite number. Let it be called as "Insignificant zeros". Zeros after decimal are considered as significant figures in physics, but here, let's don't use those Insignificant zeros for a while. Thus, let's define something

Reim's number:- A digit which is not Insignificant zero be called as Reim's number for a while. Thus a finite number has Finite Reim's numbers unlike an infinity which have Infinite Reim's numbers.

Now you can see that when we add infinite zeros to a number '22' after decimal point, doesn't change the meaning of it, thus, let's call it Insignificant zeros for a while and that's how we say that finite number has finite reim's numbers or otherwise some will say that there are infinite zeros after decimal so a finite number also have Infinite Reim's number. Yes, there are some exceptions for some finite number (like irrational, non terminating numbers) which have Infinite Reim's numbers and difference between those finite numbers and an infinity will cover in the 9th chapter.}

An Infinity has Infinite Reim's numbers (increasing number of w.r.t. unit time) and it changes from unit time to time with a positive difference from initial. A finite number has non-infinite or finite reim's number and it doesn't change from unit time to time.

Let's take a series $1 + 2 + 3 + 4 + ...$ till infinity and start summing it up. It is found that it is equal to infinity (proved *by Euler (1735), as cited in Morris Kline, 1983) and let's consider it as some infinity for a while. The first three numbers give the sum of 6 and the sum of first ten numbers are 55.*

Here the sum is increasing slowly (Here we are considering it is happening with a rate of a single sum at a unit time), and it keeps on increasing without an end. if we compare the above series summation with 1000... (In 1000... considering the rate of multiplying one 10 at a single unit time, same as the rate of each summation at a unit time), we can see that 1000...> 1 + 2 + 3 + 4 +... by logically thinking also 1000... Infinity should be greater.(Here, unit doesn't mean '1' but as the scale for this is not specified, it is said to be unit time.)

At every single moment of same unit time for both functions, if we see the answer, we will see that 1000... is greater than the series summation. Here, we can see that both are ultimately Infinities but at a unit time, it can be said that 1000... or 1000...000 (Because we can perdict that the last digit will be zero ultimately) will be greater while the operation of multiplying and summation is still not finished like Cantor when compared the two infinite sets with cardinality and conculded that there is no biggest or largest cardinal number in mathematics (Cantor, 1891).

Hence when Infinities considered with a rate, there can be bigger infinities respectively. Let's give this infinity (1000...000) a notation of 'Beta Infinity'. Beta Infinity is an example of Infinite Number.

The main question now is that what will happen if we divide 1 by Beta Infinity (it is a infinite number but question is w.r.t. rate and unit time)? The answer to this question is given by Hyperreal number system (Robinson, 1966) which is Infinitesimal number, but w.r.t. rate and unit times is:- For example, the denominator is an Infinity with some 'X' rate of increasing (here rate of increasing means increasing with unit time and not asymptotically).

We know that if the finite denominator is replaced by bigger finite number each unit time, then answer will become smaller and smaller each unit time. So if 1000... is increasing with some specific rate 'X' then the answer will also decrease with that same rate 'X'.

So the answer will become 0.000...001 (This is at Infinite unit time) where in Beta Infinity, there were infinite zeros, so in 0.000...001 there are also same infinite zeros after decimal point minus 1 (Because in this place of one '0', 1 is placed) if we see it cardinality. If we see the answer, it is an Infinitesimal number. Many people will say that this answer is neglible so it should be zero! but Infinitics deal with Infinities and numbers with indeed accuracy.

{ Infinite:- In Infinitics, Infinite is an adjective, used to describe endlessly large quantity.

Infinity:- In Infinitics, Infinity is an Infinite Number. }

As the result when people were scratching their heads about 1 upon Infinity is zero so why 1 upon 0 is not infinity but 'Not defined'! Hence if we do 1 upon 0.000...001 then the operation reverses and the answer becomes 1000...000 which is Beta Infinity. Let's give this Infinitesimal number (0.000...001) a notation of " ^0 ". ^0 is an example of Infinitesimal number.

Now, we can also define a Infinitesimal number w.r.t as "Infinitesimal number is a number which have Infinite Reim's numbers (increasing number of w.r.t. rate) (here, zeros on the L.H.S. of '1' are considered in Reim's number as these zeros change the meaning of that number and the value) and it changes from unit time to time with a negative difference from initial.

Here, if we see that when we are dividing ^0 on the both sides in the equation:- 1 / 1000...000 = 0.000...001 , when will see a expression of 0.000..001 / 0.000...001 on the right hand side which is equal to 1, as the number is divided by itself which is decreasing with same rate 'X' so at every instant of the operation or at any unit time, then will be 1 throughout and we will also see a expression of 1000...000 times 0.000...001 in the denominator of the left hand side which is again equal to 1, as if a number is increasing with a multiple of 10 at a rate 'X' and a number is decreasing with a multiple of 1/10 at a rate 'X' then their product is '1'.

Thus, we get a result of 1/1 =1 which is true. This is also the result of Non standard analysis (Robinson, 1966) which states that the product of Non fixed Infinite number (derived from reciprocal of a non fixed Infinitesimal number let's say 'S') and non fixed Infinitesimal number 'S' is always 1. About different Infinities with different rates and we will discuss on that later in detail in 4th chapter.

Now let's talk about the 0.999... equal to 1, for a while let's forget many many proofs regarding 0.999... = 1 (later we will discuss on that proofs also) and start the topic with Infinitics. From the above discussions, that ^0 is not equal to 0 if we see accurately and at every single unit time, so '1' shouldn't be equal to 0.999... because if 9 is repeating continuously without an end, at a rate (If rate is considered to 'X' for a while), there will be a difference of ^0 between the numbers 0.999... and 1. The same result is given by Hyperreal number theory (Robinson, 1966) within Non Standard system.

Now let's talk about the most common proof everyone used to prove 0.999... = 1:-

*1/3 * 3 = 1 ...(1) ,*

*And 1/3 = 0.333... therefore, 0.333... * 3 = 0.999... ...(2)*

Hence from (1) and (2) 1 = 0.999... This proof is widely used but it is wrong. If we have to divide 10 atoms to three people, there will be a remainder of 1 atom right so when we divide 1/3 constantly after decimal point there is remainder which is decreasing constantly (by logic) so, According to the remainder theorem (Euclid, 1482),

Dividend = Divisor (Quotient) + Remainder, thus,

1 = 3 (0.333...333) + 0.000...001

1 = 0.999...999 + 0.000...001

1 = 1.000...000 which is nothing but 1=1

Note that:- Now the question may arise that why the rate of decreasing remainder of the above example is considered to be equal to ^0 ? The answer to this is simple that there are infinite non-terminating numbers like 0.999... , 3.666... or 41.888... ,etc which are derived from a finite numerator and denominator.

The rate of writing the respective digit or digits after decimal point for all the non-terminating numbers will be same by logic that repetative digits (non zero digits) after decimal point for all non-terminating numbers will have same cardinality or same cardinal number till infinity thus, their remainder will also have same rate of decreasing by basic logic.

On the other hand we haven't decided or related the rate of increasing and decreasing of Beta Infinity and ^0 respectively and their number of digits to anything So we can let it be equal to the remainder's decreasing rate and the number of digits with cardinality of digits.

The above was the <u>first proof for 1 isn't equal to 0.999...</u>

Note that we haven't decided remainder's rate of decreasing with Beta Infinity's rate of increasing but Beta Infinity's rate with the remainder's rate. So in the end, remainder's rate 'X' already existed and we are making a new infinity (which is Beta Infinity)out of it with remainder's rate 'X' .Thus, ^0 , Beta Infinity and remainder of 1/3 all have same rate of repetition of a digit. Let's take <u>second proof for 1 not equal to 0.999...</u>

Wrong belief:- let x = 0.999.... and multiplying both sides by 10 then 10x = 9.999... then subtracting 'x' from both sides

then 9x = 9 so x =1 therefore, 1 = 0.999...

To answer this let's take an example of two students who were given a task of writing zeros on two different long boards and whoever wrotes as many as zeros wins. But the main thing here is that both the students have same writing speed or the same rate of writing zeros on the board so, what do we expect here? Yes, it will be a tie. But in between the competition of the writing, a third student came and did some cheating by rubbing one 0 from first student's board secretly. so now what do expect? the student will anyhow win by one more zero.

Here also it's happening the same because in 0.999...999 (the last digit of the repetition (non zero) is perdictable i.e. '9') when we multiply 10, one '9' comes before the decimal point and the number of 9's changes after the decimal point by 1 if we see it with one to one correspondence. therefore,

x = 0.999...999 multiplying it with 10 on both the sides

10x = 9.999...990 (there are infinite zeros after repetition of 9 but with consideration of cardinality of digits (non zero)after the decimal point of 0.999...999 and 9.999...990)

9x = 8.999...991 (when subtracting 0.999...999 from 9.999...990 with one to one correspondence and cardinality of repetative digits(non zero) after decimal point)

therefore, x = 8.999...991 / 9 = 0.999...999 = x

Therefore, L.H.S. = R.H.S. Here we are operating division at every unit time.

Since, we concluded that one 10 can affect the cardinality of digits somehow thus we can also say that 100/ ^0 is greater than 10/ ^0 as extra zeros will be added in the Beta Infinity as,

*100 * 100...000 > 10 * 100...000*

A question may arise here that on the left hand side, there are two zeros extra in the infinity and on the right hand side, there is one extra zero in that infinity which makes the left hand side infinity bigger than that of right hand side infinity and when compared at every single unit time.

So when we are not considering infinity with a rate then 100 * Beta Infinity and 10* Beta Infinity should both be equal? as they seem the same?

From the prespective of Cantor when two Infinite sets (like natural numbers set and Whole number set) kept in one to one correspondence then it was seen that the number of elements of Natural number set is infinite (a infinity) is actually smaller than number of elements of Whole number set, which is also infinite (a another infinity), by 1.

So here, Cantor didn't use rate in infinity to conclude that ''some infinities are bigger than other infinities'' (Cantor, 1891). Hence, when infinities not considered with rate, then same infinity is equal to same infinity and two different infinities are not equal. w.r.t. rate and without rate also. (It may be seen that at some unit time, two different infinities 'may' seem to be equal or have the same value at that unit time but aren't equal as two different infinities are compared at every single unit time and not at only a single unit time)

Thus, we can also conclude that Beta Infinity plus 3 is greater than Beta Infinity plus 1 and we can say that 2/ ^0 is greater than 1/ ^0 (Beta Infinity) as in 2/ ^0, '2' is multiplied with Beta Infinity. so, 200....000 > 100...000

Let's talk about (Beta Infinity) (Beta Infinity) or (Beta Infinity)^2, what is it? well it's another infinity but bigger than Beta Infinity. It has a rate of twice of the rate of Beta Infinity's. That means , in Beta Infinity there was multiplying one '10' at a single unit time while in (Beta Infinity)^2 there will be two '10' multiplying or multiplying one '100' at a single unit time. Hence, it has a rate of 2* 'X'. Thus we can create new Infinities which will be multiple of Beta Infinity's rate or 'X' multiple. Hence, Beta Infinity is also known as 'the basic Infinity'.*

Since we are considering infinities as a number (not as a finite number) Thus a infinity times 0 is zero and 0 divide by any infinity is also 0 (the same result was given by Robinson (1966). If we take a hypothetical example of infinity times zero is zero is, when a force is acting on a body where force is increasing at a specific constant rate but the displacement of the body is still zero and consider it will be zero at any time. So here force is equal to infinity and work on the body is zero by definition. Even if we don't consider increasing force with rate, let's say the force is Infinite acting on a body and still body isn't moving so in the end, Infinity times zero is zero.

Note that, now we have bigger Infinities than Beta Infinity (the basic infinity) like (Beta Infinity)^n (where 'n' can be anything but a positive real number and greater than 1) then the number of elements of a set of natural numbers shouldn't be beta Infinity and it can't be defined in terms of numbers and according to the Cantor, there is no greatest cardinal number (Cantor, 1891). Since we can't determine it let it be 'G' for the number of elements of Natural number set for a while. So now we can say that the number of elements of the set of integers is 2 times of 'G' + 1 since 0 is also considered as a element.

Note that we have bigger Infinities than Beta Infinity so there can be numbers who are even smaller than ^0 but very very accurately greater than 0 which can be written in the form as (^0)^n or 1/ (Beta Infinity)^n (where 'n' can be anything but a positive real number greater than 1) which will have the same mechanism like (Beta Infinity)^n of writing of zeros, after the decimal point. These derivatives of Beta Infinity and ^0 follows simple arithmetic rules.

A question may arise that why 'n' can't be less than 1? The answer is, then the rate is smaller than Beta Infinity's rate. So we get will be a Infinity but smaller than Beta Infinity and the same goes for '^0' as if the 'n' is taken less than 1 then the respective infinitesimal number which we get as a answer will be greater than ^0.

If the n is taken zero then the answer is 1 and if we take 'X' as 0 then the number given is a finite number for eg. if we take 2 as a number and take the rate of increasing as '0' then the number is not increasing and it's remains as a finite number. Let's take more examples of ^0 and the <u>third (indirect) proof</u> of 1 not equal to 0.999...

As 2/3 3 = 2 and also 2/3 = 0.666....*

*then 0.666...666 * 3 = 1.999...998*

Here we can clearly see that the last digit of this number ain't '9' (as the last digit was perdictable) so it's definitely not the case of 1.999...999 and early the mathematicians told that 0.999... and 1.999...999 is equal to 1 and 2 respectively but here the case is different! this is where they put their pens down as they thought the remainder is negligible.

Now according to the Infinitics, such divisions follows remainder theorem when 2/3 is divided first. so when we divide 2 by 3 even after decimal we get a remainder of 0.000...002 (because when we divide 2/3 by standard division we will see a remainder of 2 constantly on each step after decimal so the remainder gets smaller and smaller) therefore,

*2/3 *3 = (0.666...666 * 3) + 0.000...002*

= 1.999...998 + 0.000...002

= 2.000...000 = 2

*The fun fact here is that 0.000...002 is a derivative of ^0 by the relation of ^0 times 2. we can also slipt a finite integer into these terms such as:- we know that 3 * 2 = 6 and 2 can also be written as:- (This the fourth proof that says 1 is not equal to 0.999... but different numbers)*

*3 * (1 + 0.999...999 + 0.000...001) (as we know that 0.999...999 + 0.000...001 is 1)*

= 3 + 2.999...997 + 0.000...003

= 3 + 3 = 6 = R.H.S.

The same result can also be obtained by assuming 0.999...999 as 1 and 0.000...001 as zero but since we thought about 0.999... and 0.000...001 as different numbers, the same result is obtained which tells us that only one of the method is correct and according to the Hyperreal number system (Robinson, 1966), 0.999...999 is not equal to 1 and since standard and non standard number system are the part of mathematics and both can't give different results and due to presence of remainder of 1/3 thus, we can say that both are not equal.

<u>*Fifth proof for 1 not equal to 0.999... is as follows:-*</u>

Sum of infinite terms of G.P. series:- Sn= a (1 - r^n) /(1 - r) where n is some Infinity, and when r is less than 1 then the formula becomes a /(1 - r) ,where, r = 0.1 and a = 0.9 therefore the given is 0.9 + 0.09 + 0.009 +.... As per Infinitics, we can't approximate so when we say r^n is approaching zero continuously it doesn't mean it will be negligible or zero. The sum Sn approaches a /(1 - r) but isn't equal to a/ (1 - r). If we consider that some infinity (n) as Beta Infinity then r^n becomes equal to '^0' therefore,

Sn = 0.9 (1 - (0.1)^n) /(1 - 0.1)

= 0.9 (1 - (^0)) /(0.9)

= 1 - ^0 = 0.999.... this is the same answer we once excepted to be and now this is the proof.

If we consider n to be a different Infinity (other than Beta Infinity) then r^n will be 'like' ^0 i.e r^n will be an infinitesimal number.

Now, we can answer the question that why 1 raise to any infinity is equal to 1 and not 'not defined', as we know that infinity is hereby considered as a number (not as a finite number but as a infinite number) and we know that any infinity times zero is zero and when we apply natural log (Ln) to the both sides of the equation 1^Infinity =1 (considering L.H.S. =1 raise to infinity and R.H.S. =1)

Ln(1^Infinity) = Ln(1)

*Infinity * Ln(1) = Ln(1)*

*Infinity * 0 = 0 (as natural log of 1 is zero)*

0 = 0 , L.H.S. = R.H.S.

Hence, 1 raise to any infinity is 1 by logic and mathematically also. (Sixth proof of 1 not equal to 0.999...) Some may ask about the following assumptions for 1 raised to Infinity as follows (when x approches to infinity and by applying limits)

(1 + 1/x)^x = e

Since we concluded that 1 over infinity isn't zero but ^0(if infinity is Beta Infinity) or 'like' ^0 so,

$(1 + 0.000...001)$ ^Infinity

$= (1.000...001)$ ^ Infinity $= e$

Which is approximately equal to 'e' (As this expression gave birth (recognition) to the number 'e' still according to the rate, it is approaching to prexisting number to 'e') and 'e' is irrational and it's limit is 'e' (the result was given by Bernoulli, J., 1713) and the another expression (Seventh proof which indirectly tells the presence of Non fixed Infinitesimal number and 1 not equal to 0.999...)

$(1 + 1/x^2)$^x

gives '1' as answer by limits (A common result that can be found in any book) when x is approaching infinity. As we know that 1/ (Infinity)^2 isn't zero so, according to Infinitics, the expression tends to '1' but ain't '1'.

<u>*Another (Eighth) proof for 1 isn't equal to 0.999...999,*</u>

where we take a rectangular sheet or a piece of 2 unit square and divide the sheet's area by 2 in a sequence as shown in the figure without an end, Here many mathematicians conclude that sum of all the areas of these is 1 + ½ + ¼ + ⅛ + ... = 1.999.... is equal to 2 as initally we took a sheet of 2 unit square so L.H.S. should equal to R.H.S.

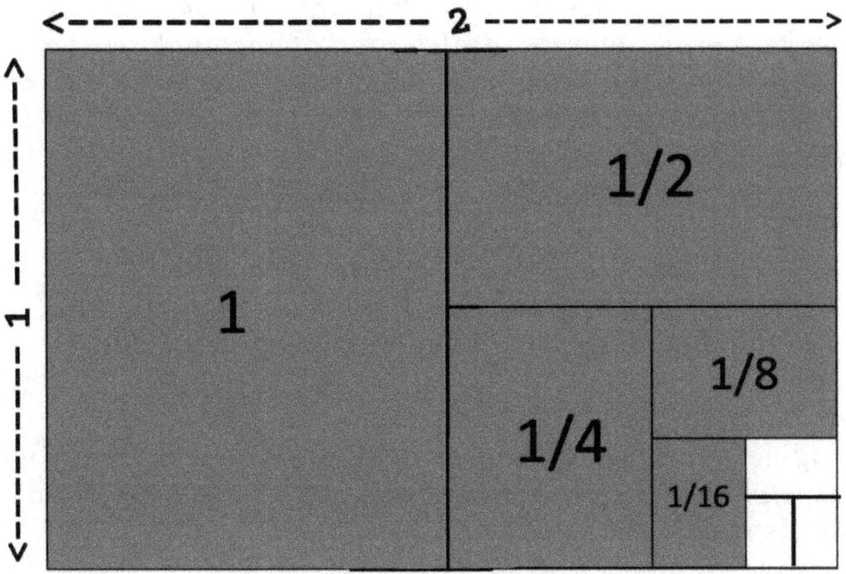

Figure 1: A Finite Area for an Infinite Series

It's like the example of ⅓, as the remainder still exist (infinitesimal ^0), suppose if we stop in between dividing ⅓ till Infinity, then the remainder is fixed very small number like 0.000000001 so in the end, when we have to get Dividend again we have to add the remainder as we can't conclude that 0.999999999 is equal to 1.

Similarly, when divide the sheet in this way and the remainder sheet remains which again undergoes division into two parts so in the end, there is always a remainder sheet which is very very small or non fixed Infinitesimal number which is to be added in the summation of the areas of parts of the given rectangle.

Thus, the summation of sequence or series 1 + ½ + ¼ + ⅛ +... is always 1.999....999 but area of rectangle is also always 2 unit square and also area of rectangle is the sum of series and the remainder (and when we see w.r.t. rate, the sum of series and the remainder at that moment of unit time).

Another (<u>Nineth</u>) proof for 1 isn't equal to 0.999....999 w.r.t. standard system, this proof is accepted worldwide,

Imagine we have endless or uncountable Alphabets (with new alphabets) and we put them each as a element in a set 'RT' as shown below:-
RT = { A, B, C, D, E, F, G, H,........}

And we have to find the probability P(1) of a alphabet picked from the RH set which is not 'A', thus P(1) = 0.9999... here we now that if A is not picked then probability isn't 1 as 'A' is also Important element of the set RH similarly we can say probability P(2) of a alphabet picked is 'A' only, so P(2) = 1 / some Infinity = some Infinitesimal number = 0.000...001 (where both are Non fixed numbers) and when we add P(1) and P(2), we get 1 (the elements of the set RH are covered) thus 1 is not equal to 0.999....

The one difference between standard numbers (real numbers) and Non standard numbers (Infinite and Infinitesimal) is that, in standard real system, 0.999... is considered to be equal to 1, as there was many old proofs regarding this and where in non standard system, 0.999... is not considered to be equal but approximately or extremely close to 1 by creating a decimal expansion which is approaching 1.

And now, with the correction in the old proofs by the Infinitics, we can say that 1 is not equal to the 0.999... in Standard real system also or mathematics is a real combination of standard and non standard numbers.

Now we can say from the above discussions that we can't (or never can) define a number which is THE closest number to '1' as there are uncountable or Infinite Number between 0.999...999 and 1 (as we can define another number which has more 9's in 0.999...999, eg 0.999...999777...777 is aslo number greater than 0.999...999 (where '999...999' and '777...777' are two Infins, about 'Infin' is in next chp))

Conclusion of this chapter:-

1) With the help of the Non-terminating number's calculation, we proved the presence of calculable Infinitesimal number (^0 and other Infinitesimals) and from that we can prove calculable Infinities exist by reciprocal of that Infinitesimal number.

2) In the world of Non fixed Infinities and Infinitesimals, we can assume a basic Infinity and Basic Infinitesimal and can use it for conventional purposes.

3) 0.999... isn't equal to 1 in Standard real system also but generally people use 0.999... = 1 for practical purpose.

4) Infinity doesn't come with a rate but considering it with rate simply our understanding towards Infinity and simply our vision into it's calculation.

5) We can compare two given Infinities or Infinitesimals in the terms of Basic Infinity's or Basic Infinitesimal's (^{0}) rate i.e. 'X'.

CHAPTER THREE

INFINS AND ERNE'S NUMBER

Let the number of zeros a Beta Infinity have, be called as 'Roh' number. I'm not talking about the zero digits which appear after decimal point or before 1 in Beta Infinity and Roh number is not a fixed number and keeps on increasing by 1 per unit time as one '10' is multiplied per unit time in Beta Infinity. ('1' is not considered for the number of digit of Beta Infinity for Roh's Number.)

__Fun Fact:-__ So, Technically, Roh's number is also a Infinity which increases by 1 each unit time but it is much smaller than Beta Infinity.

*Before we start this topic let's take an example, when we multiply 0.33 * 0.99 it gives 0.3267 as the answer but if we multiply 0.3333 * 0.9999 we get 0.33326667 as the answer, here we will notice that on the left hand side that number of digits (non zero) after decimal point is 4 for both the numbers and answer has 8 digits (non zero) after decimal point so if we increase the number of 3's and 9's equally, then the answer we have twice the number of digits (non zero) after decimal point.*

And now if we see at this equation where we have multiplied 0.333...333 and 0.999...999 so

*0.333...333 * 0.999...999 = 0.333...332666...667*

So here if we number of digits after decimal point (non zero) is twice the number of digits (non zero) of 0.333...333 after decimal point so we take two sections of this answer after decimal point as '333...332' and '666...667' , they will have same cardinality of digits (which is equal to the number of digits Beta Infinity(100...000) has or simply called as 'Roh' number).

So in this two sections 3 and 6 is repeating continously (where they are repeating till the number of digits Beta infinity (1000...000) has or Roh number, minus 1 times in each respective section, as 2 and 7 aren't repeating but still considered in the counting of the number of Digits, that's why minus 1).

So, in the result of this, in 0.333...333, there is 3 repeating the number of digits Beta Infinity has times and in 0.333...332666...667, there are two sections which have same number of elements (non zero digit) so a number can have two or more of these sections repeating till infinity (In this case, they are repeating Roh times, but it can be bigger or smaller than Roh number) (not considering 2 and 7 in terms of repetition). Let's call this section 'Infin' for a while, which 'can' have same cardinality of digits with same rate of repetition.

Here, multiplying two non-terminating numbers, give 'two sections' of repeating or 'two Infins' in the answer after decimal point and if we multiply three non-terminating numbers we get three visible Infins in the answer and so on... And it can also be done by dividing a non-terminating number by an integer also.

*For example, 1.333...333 / 3 * 3 we get 1.333...333 by cancelling 3 easily, which can also be done when 1.333...333 is divided by 3 first, then*

*= 0.444...444333...333 * 3 (here, '444...444' and '333...333' are two Infins)*

= 1.333...332999...999 + 0.000...000000...001 (here ' 333...332' and '999...999' are two Infins in 0.333...332999...999)

=1.333...333000...000 which is nothing but 1.333...333

Here, 1.333...333 /3 has remainder of 0.000...000000...001 (where '000...000' and '000...001' are two Infins) or it can be written as $(^\wedge 0)^\wedge 2$, Because w.r.t. unit time as the number of 3's in 1.333... increases, the remainder also gets smaller and smaller (you can also think it by logic).

These Infins help us to understand the calculations regarding Infinities because these two or more than two sections repeating can also be before the decimal point like an infinity:- 444...444111...111 where '444...444' and '111...111' are two Infins appearing before the decimal point.

Each Infin represents **a 'imaginary created space' for a rate of writing numbers/Digits Uncountable times** *and it's not compulsory that it will be Roh number only, as there are also bigger and smaller Infinities w.r.t. Beta Infinity thus resulting into bigger or smaller than Roh's number.*

Therefore, two Infins or more Infins 'may' contain same number of digits same as Roh number at a moment or at a single unit time or at every single unit time, with same rate of repetition of that digit.

A Infin which has a 'Imaginary created space' equal to Roh number (number of digits of the Basic Infinity (Beta Infinity) excluding 1) or a 'imaginary space' where a certain digit is repeated 'Roh number' times, is known as a 'Basic Infin'.

As there are different rates of infinities as discussed earlier like a scalar multiple of 'X', etc. Thus two Infins can have different number of spaces with two different cardinality of digits, smaller or greater than the other.

With the help of 'Infin' we can write a Non fixed Infinite and Infinitesimal number in such sections that we can represent it in the form of numbers and calculation with these non standard numbers (done in chp 4) can be seen easily but this is applicable on Infin of repeating number or digit and a Infin of non repeating number or digit can be represented in a Infin and w.r.t Basic Infin but calculations may seen difficult but not impossible.

Otherwise without the help of a Infin, Infinities or Infinitesimal's (with repeating digit or number Infins) calculation will be difficult or to write a simpler Infinity or Infinitesimal number will also be difficult as we can't write a Infinity's first till last digit without these sections and dots.

Thus, Infin helps us to see and understand the nature of the given Infinity and also shows us the last and first digit of the Infinite, Infinitesimal, irrational or non terminating number easily. They can also have two or more different Infins of different repeating digit or a number.

As above, the remainder '0.000...000000...001' has a Infin '000...000' so a question may arise that a Infin can be of zeros also? The answer is yes, we have created an imaginary space a digit/number (which can also be zero) to repeat infinite times so there are infinite zeros in the decimal point or after the number like 3.000.... and 0000789.0 has infinite zeros in the right and left side respectively so, considering infinite zeros in a 'Infin' won't harm us.

Thus, a number is surrounded by infinite Infins. It aslo helps us to compare the given Infinity with Basic Infinity or Basic Infinitesimal as per need eg. the given Infinity 1000...000 has a Infin of '000...000' which is 0.7 times rate of Basic Infin.

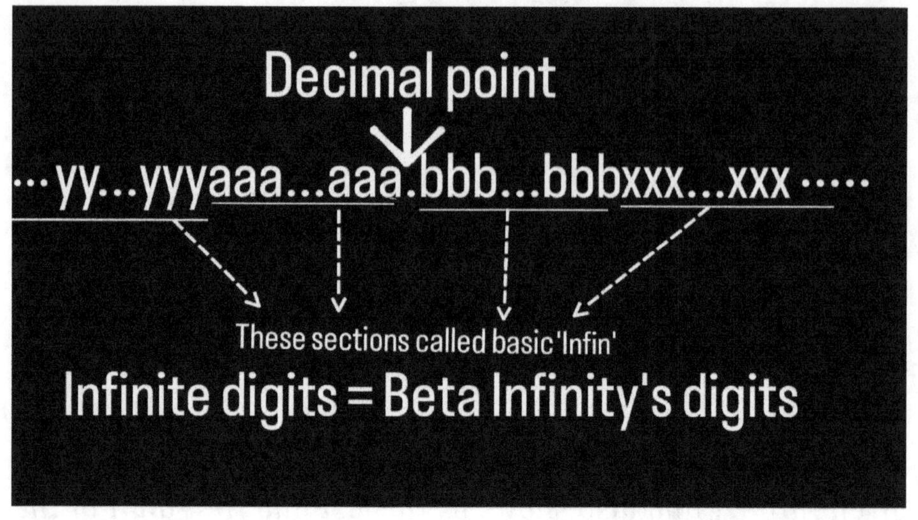

An example of Uncountable Infins of a number

Here, Beta Infinity's digits is refered to Roh's number and here Infins are considered as Basic Infin for the example, where 'a' , 'b', 'x' and 'y' can be anything but a positive integer or can be even 'zero'. Thus, a infinity number or a finite number like '2' if considered is surrounded by infinite (any type of) Infins or basic Infin i.e. '000...000'.

A Infin is a 'imaginary created space' for Uncountable digits to be placed but uncountable digits can't be placed at once so it seems like that space is also increasing w.r.t. unit time. Thus, a 'Infin' is also related with a rate.

Thus, a Basic Infin can also be defined as a Infin which has a rate of increasing of space as Roh's number increases like when roh's number is Ten million then there is a space for Ten million digits in a basic Infin and so on... So, a Infin which is not a Basic Infin, has increasing rate of space, is derived from Basic Infin's rate of increasing of space, like with a relation of number or a function multiple, etc.

*{**Fun fact:**- (10)^ Roh's number is equal to 'Beta Infinity'}*

Example, a Infin which is two times the basic Infin's rate is a Infin having a space of twice the space of a Basic Infin. As a result, we can also create a Infin having 3/2 times the space of Basic Infin i.e. in two unit time, there will be a addition of space of three digits in that Infin.

*****Note that:**- In ^0, '1' lies in the Basic Infin while in Beta Infinity, '1' doesn't lie in the Basic Infin (we can verify it by cardinality of digits and one to one correspondence of the digits).*

It aslo helps us to compare the given two Infinities with the help of (or in the terms of) Basic Infinity or Basic Infinitesimal as per need eg. the given Infinity 1000...000 has a som of '000...000' which is 0.9 times basic Infin's rate or otherwise we can compare with 'X'.

*{Here, if we can see that there can be two or more Infins in a number like 41.999...999666...666 where '999...999' and '666...666' are two Infins, the number can be or can not be considered as non terminating number as non terminating has one single digit/number or the same digit repeated throughout (**only the definition matters**) but since they are same type of Infins (having same Infin's rate and can have different or repeating digit/number) property, in Infinitics, they all comes under Erne's number which is discussed below}*

As we have seen such fractions which gives a non-terminating number as the answer but comes with a infinitesimal remainder. Such divisions can be called as 'Approx' divisions or 'Imperfect division', as the answer of the division when multiplied with the denominator doesn't give the numerator (very very accurately according to Infinitics) without adding the Infinitesimal remainder.

Let such fractions and it's answer which is non-terminating number, be called as 'Erne's numbers' for a while for better understanding while doing the operations on such fractions. And also thus there are Infinite Erne's numbers. Erne's numbers can have one or more different Infins by different repeating digit/number but all Infins of Erne's number should strictly have the same Infin's rate.

Thus, for Erne's number to occur as the answer, let 'n' be the number in the denominator which divides the numerator, and the numerator gets divided into (n + 1) parts, where 'n' parts are equal parts and one part remaining is the Infinitesimal unequal part ($\wedge 0$ or derivative of $\wedge 0$). For example, In the case of 1/3 the unequal part is '$\wedge 0$'.

According to the remainder theorem (Euclid, 1482),

*Dividend =Divisor * Quotient + Remainder ,now from this, we can have an idea when to add the remainder and when to not add, let's make some changes,*

*Dividend = Divisor * (Dividend / Divisor) + Quotient*

*Let x = Divisor and y = Dividend, therefore, y = x * y/ x + remainder thus, when y/x is an Erne's number and x is multipled (or the denominator is multiplied) remainder is added. thus, expression x * y/ x form adds up the remainder and if y /x is not an Erne's number, that means it's a perfect division and the remainder is exact zero.*

Let's take a look on the rules while dealing with Erne's number and how remainder is found for different cases:-

1) When an 'p/q' fraction is a Erne's number then if you are dividing '1/q ' first which is also an Erne's number then for the remainder to be added in the end is the remainder of '1/ q' which is Infinitesimal and to get an exact answer.

*Example, 5 / 3 = 5 * 0.333...333*

= 1.666...665 + ^0 (where 1 /3 has a remainder of ^0) (where 666...665 is a Infin)

= 1.666...665 + 0.000...001 (where 000...001 is a Infin)

= 1.666...666 = R.H.S. (where 666...666 is a Infin)

*2) If 'p / q' is not an Erne's number but '1 /q ' is an Erne's number and we are dividing ' 1/ q' first and then multiplying it with 'p' then we have to rewrite in the form of (p /q)/ q * q or y/ q * q form where y is p/ q, then the remainder of '1 /q ' (Infinitesimal) gets multiplied with y and in the end, added to it to get an exact answer.*

*Example, 6 /3 = 2 (1 /3) * 3 (here y is '2')*

*= 2 (0.333...333) * 3*

= 1.999...998 + 0.000...002 (multiplying the remainder of 1 /3 (^0) with y (2))

= 2.000...000 = 2 = R.H.S.

*Here, we have written 6 has 2 * 3 to get a form of y / q * q.*

*3) When (1/x * x) *n is the expression where 1 /x is an Erne's number and n is a real number (which can be Erne's number also) and when 1/ x is divided first then in the end the remainder of '1 /x' is multiplied with 'n' and then added to the number to get 'n' as the result.*

Example number 1, when n is not a Erne's number

*5/3 * 3 = 5 * 0.333...33 * 3 (where 'n' is 5)*

= 4.999...995 + 5 ^0*

= 4.999...995 + 0.000...005

= 5.000...000 = 5 = R.H.S.

*Here, as the remainder of 1/ 3 is ^0, so it gets multiplied with 5, i.e. 5 * ^0*

Example number 2, When n is an Erne's number

*(5 /3) /3 * 3 = 1.666...666 /3 * 3 (here, n is 5/ 3 or 1.666...666)*

*= 1.666...666 * 0.333...333 * 3*

*= 1.666...664333...334 + 1.666...666 * ^0 (here, in 1.666...664333...334, '666...664' and '333...334' are two Infins)*

= 1.666...664333...334 + 0.000...001666...666 (where, '000...001' and '666...666' are two Infins)

=1.666...666000...000 = 1.666...666 = R.H.S.

*Here, as the 'n' is 1.666...666, therefore for the remainder , it gets multiplied with the remainder of '1 /3' (^0) to get the exact answer. **Hence, A remainder can also have multiple visible Infins.***

*4) When in in (1 /x * x) * n form or (n /x * x) form, where n /x is divided first and it is an Erne's number then the remainder of 'n /x' will be directly added in the end.*

Example number 1, when n is not an Erne's number,

*5 /3 *3*

*= 1.666...666 * 3*

*= 4.999...998 + 0.000...002 (As the remainder of 5 /3 is 0.000...002 or 2 * ^0)*

= 5.000...000 = 5 = R.H.S.

Example number 2, when n is an Erne's number, if n = 5/3 = 1.666...666

*1.666...666 / 3 * 3*

*= 0.555...555333...333 * 3 (where '555...555' and '333...333' are two Infins)*

= 1.666...665999...999 + 0.000...000000...001 (where in 1.666...665999...999, '666...665' and '999...999' are two Infins and in 0.000...000000...001, '000...000' and '000...001' are two Infins) (Here 1.666... /3 has a remainder of 0.000...000000...001 or (^0)^2)

= 1.666...666000...000 = 1.666...666 = R.H.S.

Note:- *Case 1st and 2nd are almost same and case 3rd and 4th are for the same form but doing the operations on the numbers in sequence is different.*

A number having two or more different Infins (by different number repeating) and have different Infin's rate are not considered as Erne's number. Still it's a number which can be classified or not as a different non terminating number.

Conclusion of this chapter:-

*1) When considering with given two Infinities or Infinitesimals with rate, '**Infin**' tells us the repeating units in a Infinity or Infinitesimal and there can 'Uncountable' different or similar Infins following each other.*

2) Without the help of a Infin, Infinities or Infinitesimal's (with repeating digit or number Infins) calculation will be difficult or to write a simplier Infinity or Infinitesimal number will also be difficult as we can't write a Infinity's first till last digit without these sections and dots. Thus, Infin helps us to see and understand the nature of the given Infinity w.r.t. rate and also shows us the last and first digit of the Infinite, Infinitesimal, irrational or non terminating number easily (with or without rate). They can also have two or more different Infins of different repeating digit or a number.

3) Some basic principles are to be followed while dealing with Erne's number's calculations mentioned in the above cases.

CHAPTER FOUR

CALCULATION WITH DIFFERENT INFINITIES

*As we know that other Infinities can be generated from basic Infinity and ^0 by the relation of (Beta Infinity)^n or n * Beta Infinity or 1 /(^0)^n or 1 /(n * ^0), etc.*

Example, (Beta Infinity)^3 i.e. (100...000)^3 = 100...000000...000000...000 (where Infin '000...000' is repeated twice and a Infin of '000...001' is there)

*And 7 times Beta Infinity i.e. 7 * 100...000 = 700...000*

and 1 / (^0)^4 = 100...000000...000000...000000...000 (where Infin '000...000' is repeated four times and Infin of '100...000' is there)

*and 1 / (2 * ^0) = 50...000 (where the number of actual digits is Roh's number minus 1)*

There can be other Infinities like which have 9 repeating infinite times i.e. 999...999.0 (999...999 or 999...) (where 9 is repeating after decimal point)

If there are two different rates in two different Infinities 1000... to be added, then it is sure that one of them is bigger than the other and if the rates are 2 'X' and 3 * 'X' and then we can write the answer in three Infins as shown:-*

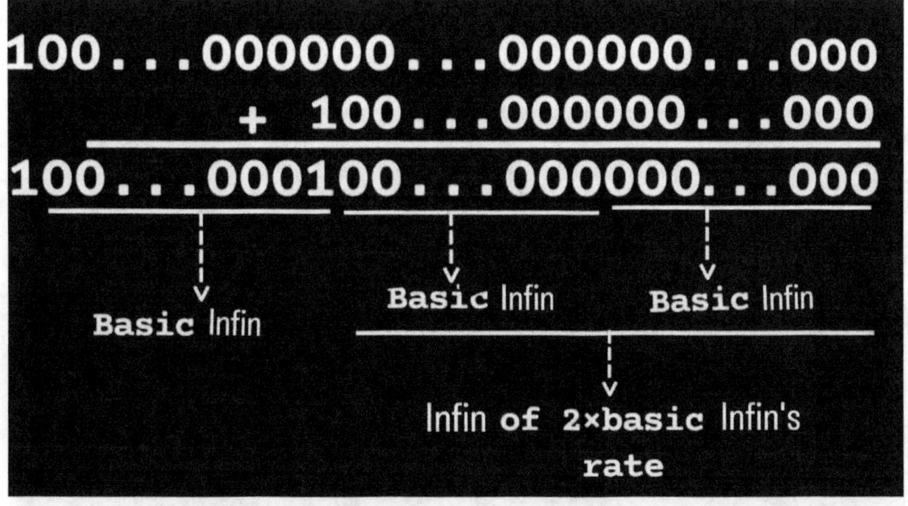

Addition between two different Infinities

Here, we can write a Infin with rate of two zeros at unit time instead of writing basic Infins twice and it is easier. But in the case of fractional rate like 3/2 or 5/3, etc if we split these rates into two or more Infins but in the terms of basic Infins then it would difficult to understand but it is possible.

Example summation of two infinities 1000... having rate 3 zeros and 3/2 zeros at a unit time respectively (3/2 zeros at a unit time doesn't really clarify much so think of 3 zeros per two unit time).

As the first Infin is having rate of 3/2 zeros per unit time. But in the second Infin remaining is having a rate which is difference of the two rates which is 3 - 3/2 = 3/2 so the rates can be shown as below.

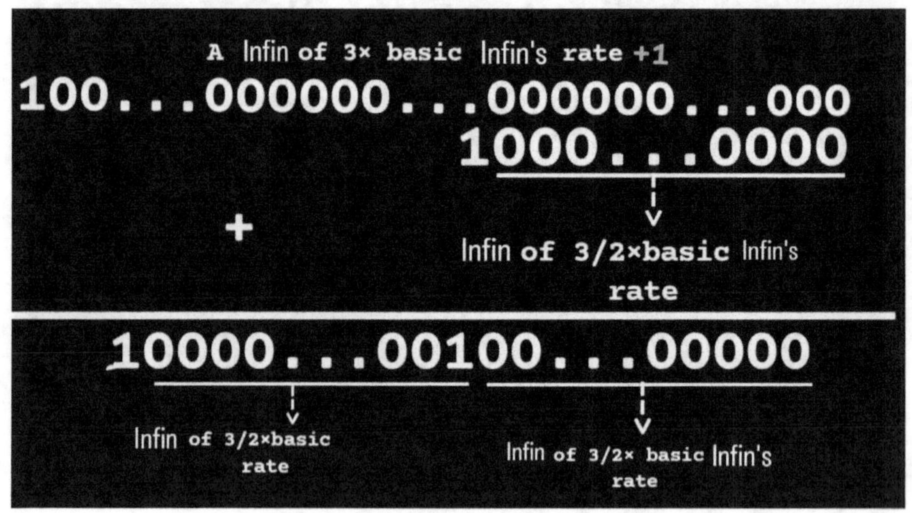

Addition between two different Infinities

Here, as the Basic Infin doesn't contain 1 for a space, thus A Infin of 3 times Basic Infin's rate +1 can be written for the Infinity 100...000000...000000...000.

*When subtracting two Infinities with different rates, the Infins can be found by the same method above but the repeative digits will change. example 3 * 'X' 1000... infinity* *minus 2 * 'X' 1000... infinity as shown below:-*

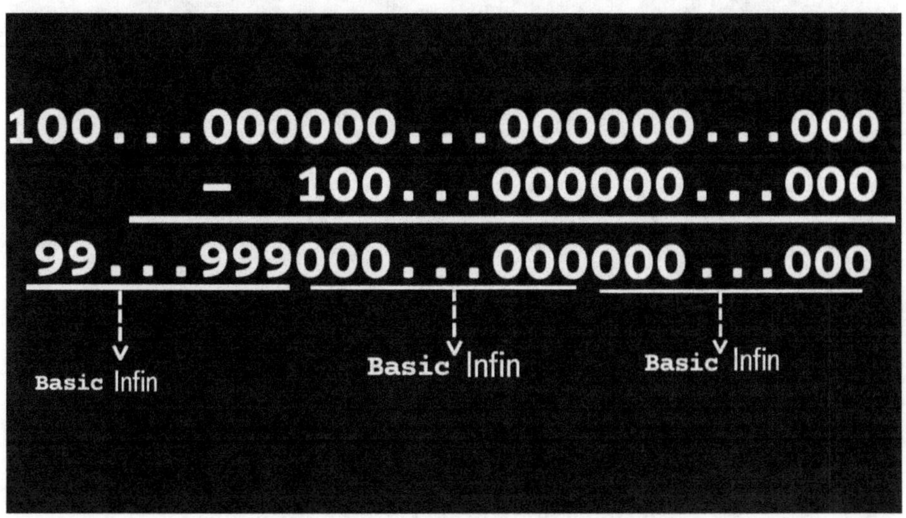

Substraction of two different Infinities

Here, in the L.H.S. first Infin of '999...999', there won't be a digit less as '1' was not considered as digit in the basic Infin, it was considered as an extra digit from the start.

When two different rates of writing same digit of Infinities are multiplied then the resultant's rate of writing is the sum of the two rates example if a infinity 1000... has a rate of 3 zeros at a unit time and a Infinity 1000... has a rate of 2 zeros per unit time is multiplied, then the resultant infinity 1000... has a rate of 5 zeros per unit time. Here we can see the numbers as follows:-

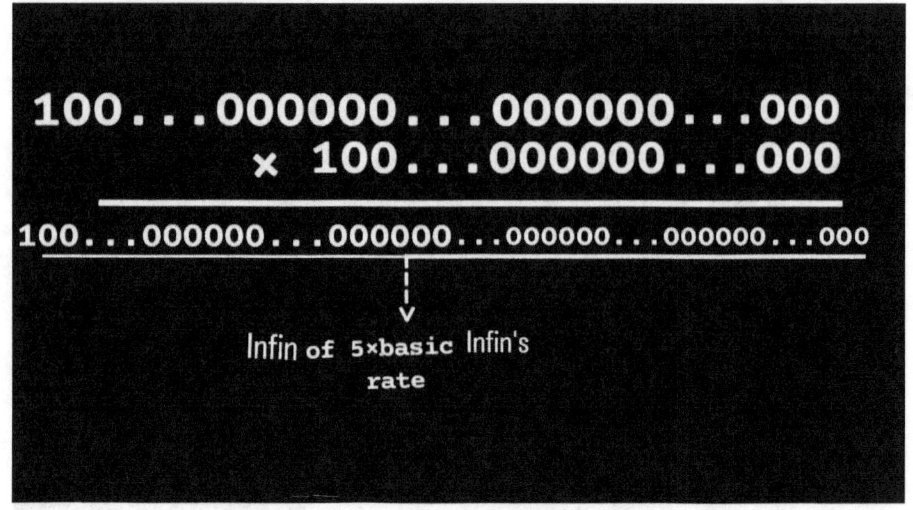

Multiplication of two Different Infinities

Here, 1 in the answer is not considered as a digit in Infin of 5 Basic Infin's rate. This is also applicable to fractional rates like rates 3 and 3/2 of Infinity 1000... thus the resultant infinity 1000... will have a rate of 9/2.*

Thus, In the result, we can compare two different Infinities w.r.t a (with considering a) same unit time (whether the other Infinity has a rate very very different from the basic Infinity or not).

As said with the help of 'Infin' we can write a Non fixed Infinite and Infinitesimal number in such sections that we can represent it in the form of numbers and calculation with these non standard numbers (done in this chp) can be seen easily but this is applicable on Infin of repeating number or digit and a Infin of non repeating number or digit can be represented in a Infin and w.r.t Basic Infin but calculations may seen difficult but not impossible.

Conclusion of this chapter:-

1) For simpler looking Infinities, the calculations seems to be simple, but for different or complex Infinities, we have to rely on it's increasing pattern and observe the answer with precision.

CHAPTER FIVE

ERNO'S NUMBER

As we now know that, Erne's number is non-terminating number as answer which later converts to the numerator of the Erne's number when multiplied by it's denominator. when 1.666...666 which is 5 /3, is multiplied with 3 its gives 4.999...998 but now we have to add it's remainder.

What if I want 4.999...998 as a number for some purpose? And I know that every existing number has a fraction or can be written in terms of a fraction. But a number can also exist in it's form without any fraction.

Thus, Infinitics conclude that a non terminating number should have a notice that whether it is derived from a fraction or not. For Example, if we are getting an area of a graph of exact 0.333...333 (where 333...333 is a Infin) and we have to use three times the area of the graph for something. so we should get 0.999...999 as an answer and not 1 because 0.333...333 can also be written as 1/3 and 1/ 3 times 3 is 1.

1/3 is an Imperfect division which gives 0.333...333 with a remainder which is hidden until a '3' is multipied to it and hidden remainder is added. but here, area of the graph is *not calculated from 1/3 but from simple summation method which has no hidden remainder!*

Thus, every non-terminating number have a fraction and it is equal But every Non-terminating numbers has it's own identity to perform operations and it should be mentioned that this non-terminating number has it's own identity, Let's call such numbers which has it's own identity for the respective/given operation as **'Erno's numbers'.**

Thus although 0.999...999 (where 999...999 is a Infin) is very very close to 1 but isn't 1 and we can't equal it to 1 by saying it's approximately equal and it won't affect so much in real life, which is true but mathematically very very accurately it is incorrect.

Thus Infinitics deals with Infinitsimal and Infinite numbers very very accurately to derive such meanings that some numbers are different. Therefore, A number derived in the presence of an remainder and a pure existing number which is not derived form any fraction and without having an hidden remainder <u>is the difference between Erne's number and Erno's numbers</u> yet they seem the same but different according to the Infinitics.

Conclusion of this chapter:-

*1) The difference between Erne's number (fraction) and Erno's number, though it is the same number **yet difference of the hidden remainder.***

2) We should describe or indicate whether a non terminating number is derived from a fraction or not.

CHAPTER SIX

ALPHA INFINITY/ NOT DEFINED

Alpha Infinity is not a Infinity but contains 'Infinity' in it's name only.

Before starting this topic, understand that 0/0 or 1/0 don't follow multiplication and division conversion law. and if we are doing this then we are concluding that 0/0 is '1'! so the assumption and statements that "0/0 could be anything" "As 0 times anything is zero", both statements are correct but this reason is wrong for this and zero going from denominator to the R.H.S. numerator for multiplication is wrong.

And also zero doesn't follow the rule of power i.e. $a^m / a^n = a^{(m-n)}$ because a shouldn't be equal to zero or otherwise it is concluding that 0/0 is 1 or we can say that $0/0 = 0^4 / 0^2 = 0^{(4-2)} = 0^2 = 0$ but this wrong so it doesn't follow indices rule of power. hence we can't derive 0^0 from 0/0 hence, 0^0 and 0/0 if exist there are totally different expressions.

People may ask that "Can't these two different expressions may have the same answer Infinity?" The answer is yes but we will ask which Infinity? Because there are infinite Infinities! out there and according to the Cantor, there is no "biggest Infinity" as there is no largest cardinal number. (Cantor, 1891) so it can't be Infinity.

And the property "when the denominator are same or the numerators are same of same fraction then the numerators or denominators are also same respectively" this is only applicable when the denominator is non zero like 2/3 = 2/3 so multiplying by 3 on both sides. so we get 2 =2 but in 1/0 = 2 /0 multiplying it with 0, but 0/0 doesn't cancels to give 1 so that 1 = 2.

So we should stop this that why 1/0 = 2/0 so when denominators are same, then numerators should also be equal but 1 isn't equal to 2 so that's why its 1/0 is 'not defined'. I know it is 'not defined' but we should stop applying this property to zeros in the denominator.

By the definition of Imperfect Divisions that when the fraction is an Erne's number then it tries to divide the numerator equally in parts but fails with a infinitsimal remainder so when we look at 1/0 it does seem that the denominator will try to divide 1 into '0' parts (which is impossible to think but still) but anything times zero is zero, so it may have infinite or uncountable answers but still the remainder is 1 whatsoever.

In '0/0' also it tries to divide the numerator and it is successful as anything times zero is zero so it also gives infinite answers and the remainder is zero.

As for now, we know that 1/0 can't be Infinity in any way. As per the limits, the answer approaches to infinity or negative of an Infinity, whenever the denominator is close to zero which is true yet some concludes that it is Infinity, similarly for 0^0 is 1 (but it isn't). As per Infinitics, we have to be more sure about the answer rather than depending on the limits and approximately to the closest number.

so when an expression can give infinite answers i.e. all real numbers including infinities and a function can only have a single unique element then Let's call it's answer as 'Alpha Infinity' (i.e. 'not defined') for a while as something's unknown as it contains infinite answers yet it is something not specified like there are infinite possibilities/answers or like something's "Not Defined" at the moment.

*In short, **Not Defined is Alpha Infinity** but it is renamed, as 0/0 and 1/0 seems to have infinite answers.*

Now since we can't write 0/0 as 0^0 or viceversa yet they have the same answer i.e. Aplha infinity. While dealing with 2^n where 'n' is a natural number while we see that unnoticeable multiplicative factor is 1 but in 0^0 or in 0/0 the unnoticeable multiplicative factor can be anything thus this can also be a reason why 0^0 or 0/0 can't be 1 and why it is Alpha infinity.

A practical example for the Alpha infinity is if we are calculating a speed or velocity for an particle which is given by s = distance covered / time taken so at time =0 and distance = 0, the speed can't be determined as it will be 'seen' at rest so if we are seeing a particle in an instant of time like time has paused. so we can't be sure that what's it's speed will be so there are infinite possibilities of speed that a particle can have thus it's Alpha infinity (something not defined). And we know that tan 90 degree is 1/0 is Alpha Infinity (Not defined).

Another perfect example for a 'Function' equal to 0/0 and still logically having Infinite answers, The slope for a given isolated single point is 0/0 as there is no change in x and y axis, then the slope could be anything from negative Infinity to postive Infinity (as Tan 90 degree is also Alpha Infinity i.e. seems to have Infinite answers) but could be any one of those for a given point!

Now the question is 'Do slope of x-axis and y-axis's product is -1'? The answer will be a new yes IF 0/0 is 1 and which is not possible so it's not. And 'IF' 0/0 is 1 then which one will have the negative slope? Let's dig into it, we always indicate x1, x2 and y1, y2 on the coordinate system randomly which gives a result that it can be both postive or both negative or one of them is negative.

If we have a imaginary straight line going from top left to bottom right in the coordinate system, which will indicate which will be x1, y1 and x2, y2 by the line which touches one of the points first.

From this orientation, we get an result that slope of x-axis (without any rearrangement of the sign) is positive and slope of y-axis (without any rearrangement of the sign) is negative.

What if we take that imaginary straight line from bottom left to top right, then we get an result that slope of x-

axis (without any rearrangement of the sign)is negative and slope of y-axis (without any rearrangement of the sign) is positive. So, it "can" or "may" be that slopes of x and y axes exist simultaneously positive and negative for each other i.e. when slope of x-axis is positive then slope of y-axis is negative and viceversa.

As many slopes which are not parallel or is x and y axes, are determined by randomly or following a straight vertical line from left to right or right to left (and when this line touches two points at once then we run a horizontal line from top to bottom or bottom to top and it only happens in the case of y-axis) and every line (except y axis)are not parallel to this line.

So what if this could be the problem that why slopes of x and y axes are sometimes all positive or negative w.r.t. to this vertical line and horizontal line? so let's consider that they are positive and negative for each other for a while.

For x axis, the slope is 0 which in the earlier form was 0/x where 'x' can be anything. and for y axis, the slope is x/0 where 'x' can be anything. let's assume 'x' for both the slopes be the same (only magnitude) for a while. (which is not complusory but for the sake of calculations), Thus, their slope's product will be:-

x /0 * 0/x = (-1 /0) *0 (As slopes of x and y axes "can" or "may" be exist simultaneously positive and negative for each other but let's consider it opposite w.r.t. for a while)

*And here if we apply remainder theorem as it is in the form of y /x *x,*

*-1 /0 * 0 = Alpha Infinity * 0*

= 0 + (-1) = -1 (here -1/0 is divided first and the remainder of this is '-1', thus in the end '-1' is added)

*It seems to follow the two perpendicular lines slope's product rule which is equal to '-1'. But as said that it happens IF 0/0 is 1 only! and also remainder theorem and Erne's remainder adding rule is only applicable when the denominator is non zero or in the form y /x *x where, x cancels x to give 1 so this is not the case of 0/0 and anytime when we multiply Alpha Infinity with something (even zero) it gives Alpha Infinity (Not defined) as answer and we also assumed that 'x' is both slopes are same (magnitude) which is not true in all cases as we can take any far away points on the axes. So however in the end, their slope's product is Alpha Infinity or Not defined.*

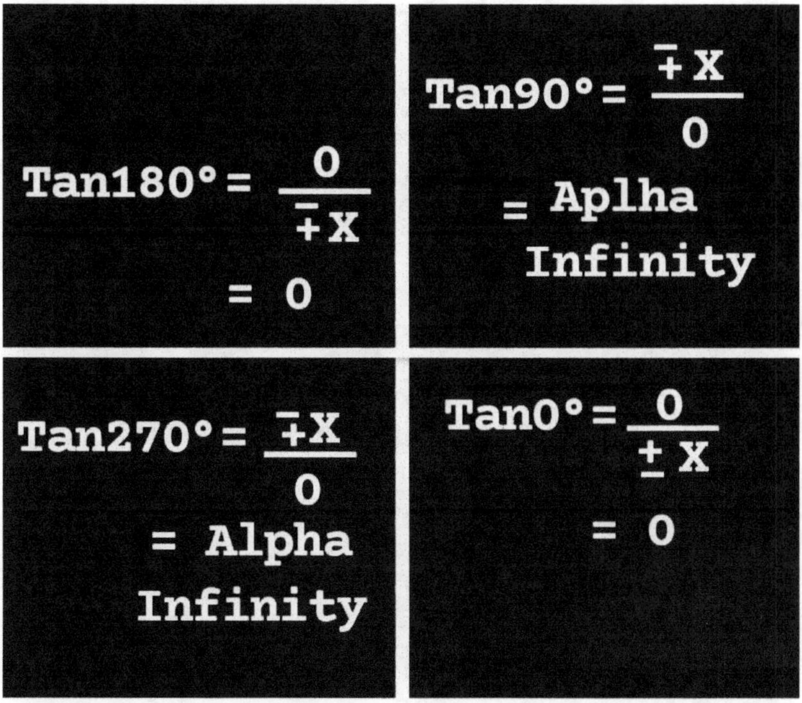

$$\text{Tan}180° = \frac{0}{\overline{+}X} = 0$$

$$\text{Tan}90° = \frac{\overline{+}X}{0} = \text{Aplha Infinity}$$

$$\text{Tan}270° = \frac{\overline{+}X}{0} = \text{Alpha Infinity}$$

$$\text{Tan}0° = \frac{0}{\pm X} = 0$$

Different values for Tan theta at critical points

The above figure shows different values of tan theta at 0, 90, 180 and 270 degrees where 'x' could be anything but a real number. Which will ultimately give 0, Alpha Infinity, 0 and Alpha Infinity as the answer respectively.

So 0/0, 1/0, 2/0, 3/0,..... all give Alpha Infinity as answer (they have different remainder but it doesn't matter because anything multiplies or divides with Alpha Infinity gives Alpha Infinity in the end) and Reciprocal of Alpha Infinity or 1/0 doesn't give 0 answer as zero doesn't cancels out to be in numerator.

Want to dive deeper into Alpha Infinity? I break it all down in my latest paper:

Ratnani, G. (2026). Infinitics: Everything's Relative in the Existence and True Nature of 'Undefined'. Zenodo. https://doi.org/10.5281/zenodo.18822379

Conclusion of this chapter:-

1) Not Defined and Infinities are not the same thing as some people conclude that they are the same thing.

2) Some properties of 'Zero' mentioned above are to be remembered.

CHAPTER SEVEN

THE CALCULATIONS OF INFINITIES WITH CONSTANTS

1) Alpha infinity times 'a' or Aplha Infinity divides by 'a', where 'a' is a real number (even zero and any infinity) gives Alpha Infinity as the answer. Even Alpha Infinity times Alpha Infinity is Alpha Infinity.

2) Beta Infinity times 'a' where is a is non zero real number (But it shouldn't be anything between or equal to negative $^\wedge 0$ to positive $^\wedge 0$ (except zero), gives rise to new infinity (if 'a' is negative then negative of a infinity and if 'a' is positive then a positive infinity).

3) Beta Infinity times 'a' where is between negative $^\wedge 0$ to positive $^\wedge 0$ (except zero), gives rise to new negative and positive Infinitesimal numbers respectively. And when 'a' is equal to negative and positive $^\wedge 0$ then the answer is -1 and 1 respectively.

Thus, any Infinity times 'a' gives new infinities where 'a' shouldn't be in between or equal to negative 1/ that infinity to positive 1/ that infinity.

4) Beta Infinity times zero is zero thus any infinity times zero is zero.

5) Beta Infinity divides by 'x' where 'x' is a real nonzero number (but positive 'x' shouldn't be greater than or equal to Beta Infinity and negative 'x' shouldn't be less than or equal to negative of Beta Infinity) gives rise to a new Infinity.

Thus, Any Infinity divides by 'x' where 'x' is a real non zero number (but positive 'x' shouldn't be greater than or equal to that Infinity and negative 'x' shouldn't be less than or equal to negative of that Infinity) gives rise to a new Infinity.

6) If Beta Infinity is divided with 'x' where positive 'x' is greater than Beta Infinity or negative 'x' is less than negative of Beta Infinity then the answer is some positive Infinitesimal number and negative of some Infinitesimal number respectively.

7) If Beta Infinity is divided with 'x' where 'x' is positive and negative of Beta Infinity, then the answer is 1 and -1 respectively.

Thus, Any Infinity is divided with 'x' where 'x' is greater than that Infinity or negative 'x' is less than negative of that Infinity then the answer is some positive Infinitesimal number and negative of some Infinitesimal number respectively.

And if 'x' is positive and negative of that Infinity, then the answer is 1 and -1 respectively.

Conclusion of this chapter:-

1) Everything's possible like when you deal calculations of Infinities with precision and great accuracy!

CHAPTER EIGHT

A FAMOUS INFINITE SERIES

The famous problem:- Infinity minus Infinity = Ln (2) ? (where Ln is natural log)

This question is already been solved by mathematicians but to conclude something for Infinity minus Infinity is something we will start again. As we know that there are different Infinities which have different values. This problem/question was started with a series i.e. 1 - 1/2 + 1/3 - 1/4 + 1/5 - 1/6 +.... = Ln (2) (where Ln is natural log) (A common result which can be found in textbooks)

And if we did some rearrangement of this series and divide it into two parts i.e.

1 + 1/3 + 1/5 +.... which is equal to some Infinity

and also - 1/2 - 1/4 - 1/6 - .... = Negative of some Infinity and if we add these two parts of a series we get, Infinity minus Infinity approximately equal to Ln (2),

Earlier people were not considering Infinity as a number to perform operations and considering Infinity minus Infinity as Indeterminate form as in various places in Standard real system,as the analysis of answers was not clear and they also considered as there is only one Infinity (which is just a concept) and some considered that there is Infinity with different cardinal numbers but Infinity is Infinity in Standard real system.

Now we can see that 'considering Infinity as a number with rate is very beneficial for us and we are not considering it as a finite number but as a number which has infinite digits w.r.t. a rate for calculations!'

We can't tell the exact value for this above Infinity as like Beta infinity i.e. 1000...000 where we can perdict the digits but here in the above example the number keeps on changing so the digits keeps on changing but if we perform operation per unit time for both parts of the series and subtract it we can see a number getting close to Ln (2) so that's how we do it.

And for the Infinite series 1 - 1 + 1 - 1 + 1 - 1 +..... without an end, some proofs show that it is equal to 0.5 and textbooks says it's not defined (A common result). Infinitics also concludes that it should be 'Not defined' as answer because w.r.t. rate (each operation done at a unit time) so at every unit time when it's a even unit time so the answer should be zero as even number of elements of series 1 - 1 +1 - 1 +... ends at '-1' in the end thus '0' but at every odd unit times there will be a odd number of elements of the series so it will give '1' as answer.

So that's why it's 'not defined' but we can say that it's '1' and '0' that keeps on repeating as the answer but it's 'not defined'. When spliting the series as the summation of 1 + 1 + 1 +... and 1 - 1 - 1 -... , we will always get 0 as answer at every single unit time which is inappropriate as we are indirectly doing biased two operations at each unit time.

Thus, we can conclude that infinity minus infinity or infinity plus infinity shouldn't not always be 'not defined' but a number or some infinity sometimes. Similar results can be seen in Robinson's work in 1966.

Conclusion of this chapter:-

1) Some 'A' Infinity plus 'A' Infinity isn't equal to the same 'A' Infinity but greater Infinity.

CHAPTER NINE

IS ERNE'S OR ERNO'S NUMBER A INFINITY?

Let's recall the definition of an Infinity w.r.t. a rate "Infinite number has Infinite Reim's Numbers (increases w.r.t. unit time) and it changes from unit time to time from initial, with a positive difference" and when we look at any Erne's number or any non-terminating number like 4.9999...., at every unit time, there is an increase in number of 9's in 4.999... (Erne's number).

So practically by thinking and mathematically, at every stage w.r.t. rate, the number keeps on Increasing (even if the number is increasing very slowly and all but still there's a positive difference from the initial) and ultimately Erne's number or non- terminating number also have Infinite Reim's number (as these digits can change the meaning of that number), So shouldn't Erne's number also be considered as an Infinity with some decreasing varing type in the rate of increasing ?

Like irrational numbers like 'root 2' when considered with rate, there is an positive difference w.r.t. initial and it has infinite Reim's numbers, so shouldn't irrational number also considered as Infinite number?

The excepted answer is a 'NO' as how come 4.999... be considered as a Infinite number! And the answer is also a 'NO'. The reason behind it w.r.t. rate is that a Infinite number ultimately surpass every single finite number of the number line or it will eventually surpass every single finite number, whether that unit time is very very far away or not but eventually it will.

Here, 4.999... will not surpasses '5' at any point or at any unit time. So, any Erne's number or irrational number is not an infinity w.r.t. also. Thus, the final definition for an Infinite number w.r.t. rate is that "Infinite number has uncountable Reim's number (increasing number of) and which will surpasses every single real finite number eventually irrespective of at which unit time and it changes from unit time to time for different infinite numbers but ultimately will".

You can also change the definition for a finite number w.r.t. rate by saying that it doesn't change and surpasses and all. Thus, a finite number can also have infinite Reim's number.

{Sometimes an infinity it doesn't change for 'some' unit time but eventually it will change (Rare functions which gives a Infinity as answer) which totally depends on the given function which gives the direct an Infinity. <u>As said some things come with some exceptions! which comes under complex type of Infinity where calculation is little difficult.</u>}

Conclusion of this chapter:-

*1) A number when considered with a rate and it's increasing slowly or by little, is not always an Infinity or a number with a rate and it's decreasing, is not always an Infinitesimal but **can be a simple 'Finite' number!***

CHAPTER TEN

INFINITE SETS

The question may arise that how one now can compare two sets since there is no one infinite number but many and different in sizes? and can one put different Infinities in the end or think it as the end in different Infinite sets? and does size of a set depends upon the infinity we choose to put in the end or think it as the end?

The answer is that we can't put any Infinity at the end or think of it as the end of any Infinite set or any Infinite series and not even it's symbol. And if we have to compare two 'comparable' Infinite sets, we can do it by arrange it's elements in such sequence eg. can arrange the elements in ascending or descending order and we have to put each element in one to one correspondence (method given by George Cantor, 1891) from starting.

The next step is to observe the elements if the values of the first infinite set are getting bigger and bigger w.r.t. second infinite set then the first infinite set has lesser elements w.r.t. second infinite set.

We can't compare two Infinite sets having non comparable elements unless and until they have a relation between them, for example, Infinite sets of Alphabets and numbers have non comparable elements but if there is a condition given which gives a relation between numbers and alphabets then we can compare which will be difficult but not impossible.

Example, let set A = {1, 2, 3, 4, 5,...} and set B = {4, 8, 16, 20, 24,...} and given two Infinite sets have comparable elements. The values of Infinite set B is getting bigger and bigger, thus Infinite set B has lesser number of elements w.r.t. Infinite set A. The comparsion of two Infinite sets with one to one correspondence or 'Bijection' of elements is already given by George Cantor in 1891.

*Or we can plot the comparable elements sets on a suitable graph with **'n'th element on the x-axis and the value on the y-axis** with suitable scale for the comparsion, then we can join the points and observe, which curve or the structure has the greater slope has lesser elements w.r.t. another Infinite set.*

Similarly, we can compare two Infinite series summation or two Infinite or Infinitesimal numbers using graph with unit time on the x-axis and size of the Infinite or Infinitesimal at that moment on y-axis with suitable scale.

Example, if we have two Infinities:- Beta Infinity with the function of 10 raise to Roh's Number and 'J' Infinity + 1 (where let's say J Infinity is summation of the Infinite series:- 1+1+1+1+...) and comparing these two Infinities with the help of graph shown as below, where the line close to y axis represents 10 raise to Roh's number Infinity and straight line represent 'J' Infinity + 1.

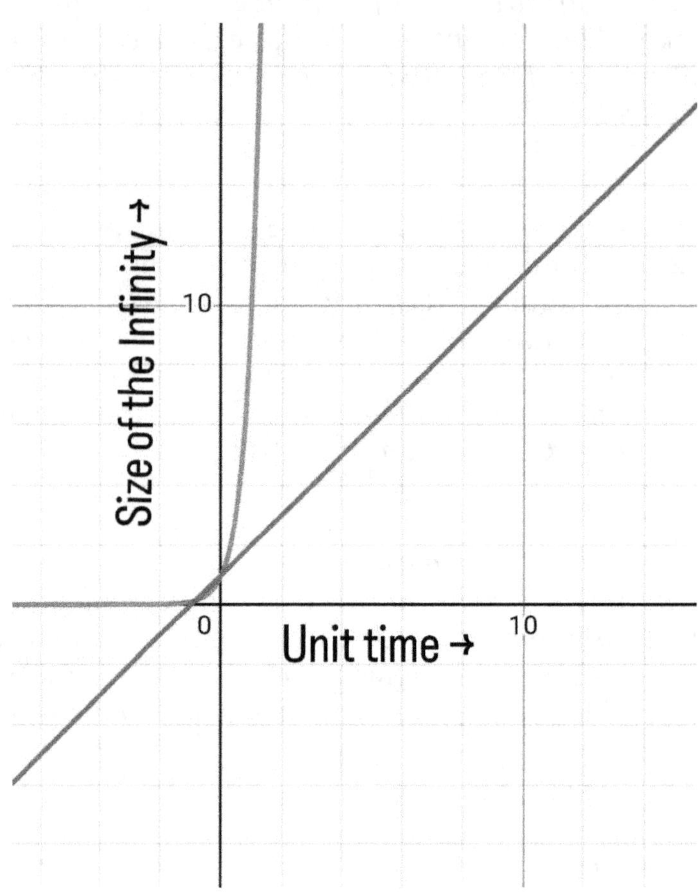

Graph of two Infinities

Here, we can clearly see that slope of Beta Infinity is large w.r.t. Infinity 'J' +1 Thus, Beta Infinity is larger than Infinity 'J' +1 (Excepted answer by logically thinking was also Beta Infinity)

Conclusion of this chapter:-

1) We can compare two Infinite sets (having comparable elements) whether with the help of graph or not.

67

Conclusion

Even though it's wild to think of an Infinite, Non-terminating number and Infinitesimal number with a rate but it doesn't truly exist with a rate but as you can see that it has various applications in the fields of the Mathematics by only considering it with a rate and it proves that Infinity is a number but we can't perform calculations in the form of numbers or it is complex to do without considering it with a rate.

Glossary

Cardinal number:- A whole number which can be counted like 1,2,3,... etc. that represents a quantity.

Cardinality:- The cardinality is the number of elements in a set or in something else.

Infinitesimal:- Something that is extremely small or smaller than any feasible measurement, but it is not in size.

Standard numbers:- Real Numbers

Non standard numbers:- The additional numbers/elements (Infinite and Infinitesimal)

Asymptotic:- Behaviour of a function which often results to a Non fixed infinite number or basically a Infinity.

Bijection:- One to one correspondence of elements of two mathematical sets which have uncountable elements.

References

1] Bernoulli, J. (1713). Ars Conjectandi. Basel: Thurneysen Brothers

2] Cantor, G. (1891) On a elementary question in the theory of manifolds. Translated by W. Ewald. In Ewald (1996), vol. 2, pp. 920-2.

3] Euclids, Euclid's elements, Book 7, Augsburg, Erhard Ratdolt, 1482-05-25 Hypsicles, of Alexandria Contributor. Mocenigo, Giovanni, 1408-1485 Dedicatee.

4] Euler and infinite series. Morris kline Mathematics Magazine, vol. 56, No. 5. (nov., 1983), pp. 307-314.

5] Robinson, A. (1966). Non-standard analysis. North-Holland Publishing.

Want To Explore More Of Infinitics?

If the concepts in this book have sparked your curiosity and you want to dive even deeper into the mathematics and philosophy of Infinity, there is a wealth of literature waiting for you!

For readers interested in the advanced calculations and theoretical frameworks discussed in these chapters, I highly recommend exploring the following papers:

1] Ratnani, G. (2025). INFINITICS: NOMENCLATURE, CLASSIFICATION AND CALCULATION OF THE HYPERREAL NUMBERS. Zenodo. https://doi.org/10.5281/zenodo.17435830

2] Ratnani, G. (2025). INFINITICS: RATE CONCEPT WITHIN AN INFINITE SET. Zenodo. https://doi.org/10.5281/zenodo.17435063

3] Ratnani, G. (2026). Infinitics: High Order Infinities/ Infinitesimals. Zenodo. https://doi.org/10.5281/zenodo.18822618

4] Ratnani, G. (2026). Infinitics: Everything's Relative in the Existence and True Nature of 'Undefined'. Zenodo. https://doi.org/10.5281/zenodo.18822379

www.ingramcontent.com/pod-product-compliance
Lightning Source LLC
Chambersburg PA
CBHW050801160726

48004CB00002B/652